YETI doesn't like SPAGHETTI

Written by: Heather Parker

Illustrations by: Emily Doolittle

This book is dedicated to
my husband and children.

May you always know that you are
loved more than there are fish in the
sea, and stars in the sky.

This is Yeti.

Yeti does NOT like spaghetti.

Yeti is a goldendoodle who will eat
ALMOST ANYTHING from A to Z....

...but this DOODLE won't eat
ANY NOODLES.

Spaghetti is slimy, squirmy, squishy
...and it makes Yeti SICK.
He won't even take one LICK...ICK!

But...

Yeti will eat...
Apple cores,
Body pillows,
Corn Cobs,
and Dirty Diapers!

But, if you throw a piece of spaghetti his way, he will run away like he is being chased by a *venomous* VIPER!

Yeti will scarf down **E**gg shells,

Fondant **F**rosting, **G**ift boxes, **H**air ties,

and even the paper off your **I**ce cream CONE.

But when you put a bowl of spaghetti on the floor, it will make him roll over and MOAN.

He devours **J**igsaw puzzles,

   Kalamata olives,

      Lawn gnomes made from wood,

         Mangos, a **N**ew Shoe,

           and an **O**ld SHOE too!

But, ask him to eat just one bite of spaghetti,

and it is like he is being given

cherry cough medicine when he has the FLU.

Yeti swallows **P**acifiers,
  Quiche lorraine, **R**adishes,
   Sponges, **T**in foil,
    Underwear (clean or dirty!),

Vienna sausage, **W**rapping paper,

X-mas cookies for Santa,

Yarn, and **Z**oo animal TOYS.

But what if there were meatballs in the

spaghetti...

would Yeti still be COY?

Oh no, no, no...

he ate it...

faster than he would eat TWINE.

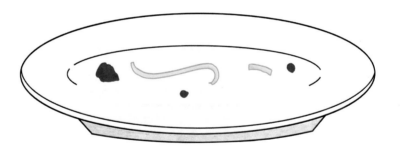

He ate all the spaghetti with meatballs....

He even ate MINE!

Yeti is now a goldendoodle who eats ~~almost~~ EVERYTHING from A to Z
...even noodles!

So... Yeti does like spaghetti after all

....OH YETI!

Glossary:

- Goldendoodle: a golden-retriever and poodle mix.
- Venomous: toxic or poisonous.
- Viper: a fanged poisonous snake.
- Fondant: a thick decorating frosting.
- Coy: shy.
- Twine: strong string twisted together.

The Inspiration:

Yeti is our goldendoodle. The funny yet SCARY truth to this alphabet story is that Yeti has truly eaten all of these things! He seems to find his way into mischief on a regular basis despite our efforts to keep him safe. A common way we describe Yeti when we are asked how he is doing is… "Yeti is trying his best!" ---which means: he is trying to be on his best behavior, but often isn't. We love him for the dog he is, and all he eats!

ISBN 978-1-66783-521-1